COME TO THE LIGHT

Retreat/Companion WORKBOOK

RICHARD T. CASE

To my wife, Linda, who has been a "shining" example of living in the Light—the truth, the way of God for us—and having the discernment to understand and avoid darkness. God has revealed to us how significant this is to living the Covenant life, the abundant life, that He has planned for us. We live in a dark world and in the natural it is easy to compromise our decisions and activities in that dark place. He is Light and He provides the way for us to always live in this life—and the focus is truth. Linda has been faithful throughout all our decisions and activities to help us pursue truth and to stand on the truth revealed. Living in the Light with Linda (LLL) has been a true joy and I am privileged to have such a wonderful partner. She is truly a woman of strength and courage that seeks to live in the Light.

Acknowledgments

We wish to thank all of the leaders of our **Ministry: Living Waters—ABIDE Ministries!** These leaders have also learned what it means to live in the Light and receive discernment of darkness—and not to compromise for convenience but to always seek His way of Light. And as in all of their covenant life (blessed to be a blessing) they are now all giving this away to others—who then are learning to live in the Light and not compromise with darkness—Thank you all:

These leaders are:

Jake & Mary Beckel
Joe & Leigh Bogar
Rich & Janet Cocchiaro
Larry & Sherry Collet
Scott & Kristen Cornell
David & Melissa Dunkel
Tom & Susanne Ewing
Rick & Kelly Ferris
Joel & Christina Gunn
Scott & Terry Hitchcock
Chris & Jaclyn Hoover
Rick & Nancy Hoover
Tad & Monica Jones
Ed & Becky Kobel
Don & Rachelle Light
Chris & Heidi May
Terry & Josephine Noetzel
Steve & Carolyn Van Ooteghem
Preston & Lynda Pitts
Dan & Kathy Rocconi
Bob & Keri Rockwell
John & Michelle Santaferraro
Allyson & Denny Weinberg
Neal & Kathy Weisenburger

COME TO THE LIGHT: RETREAT/COMPANION WORKBOOK
PUBLISHED BY LIVING WATERS—ABIDE MINISTRIES
7615 Lemon Gulch Way
Castle Rock, CO 80108

Unless otherwise noted, all Scripture quotations are from the ESV® Bible (The Holy Bible, English Standard Version®), copyright © 2001 by Crossway Bibles, a publishing ministry of Good News Publishers. Used by permission. All rights reserved.

ISBN: 978-0-578-34284-9
Copyright © 2024 by Richard T. Case.

All rights reserved. No part of this publication may be reproduced, distributed or transmitted in any form or by any means, including photocopying, recording, or other electronic or mechanical methods, without the prior written permission of the publisher.

Publisher's Cataloging-in-Publication data

Names:
Title:
Description: .
Identifiers: ISBN | LCCN
Subjects:

Printed in the United States of America 2024 — 2nd ed

TABLE OF CONTENTS

Lesson One:
Understanding Light vs. Dark: What is Light?. 2

Lesson Two:
What Dose the "Light" Provide? What is Our Role?. 12

Lesson Three:
What is Our Role? (Continued) 42

Lesson Four:
What is Our Role? (Continued) 32

Lesson Five:
Results of "Walking in the Light" and Our Call To "Give it Away". 42

LESSON 1:
UNDERSTANDING LIGHT VS. DARK: WHAT IS LIGHT?

> "But remember, to understand light, we do need to realize we live in a dark world."

Why is understanding "light" so important?

One answer may be obvious: because we live in a dark world.

This course is called "Come to the Light" and will be a salve to those of us who find ourselves in the dark, confusing world where it seems that, culturally, everything is falling apart. This course will help lead us to understanding how, even in this darkness, we are called to live as a believer or true light in this world. To do this, we must first recognize there is a spiritual dimension to our life. We don't just live in the natural. And behind that spiritual dimension is the battle between the light, the true life of God in the Spirit, and the darkness, which is the life of the enemy, the satanic and demonic.

Once we understand this, we are quickly able to discern what is true, what is light, and what is coming from God—His wisdom will never be confused with the darkness. This course will take us into the depth of this and will reveal discernment, truth, light, and how we are to be led into the abundant life that God has for us.

But remember, to understand light, we do need to realize we live in a dark world.

In John 10:10, we see a description of the enemy. Describe the enemy's nature as revealed here. How does this impact the world we live in, and why this is important to understand regarding our life?

> **Read John 10:10:**
>
> **10** The thief comes only to steal and kill and destroy. I came that they may have life and have it abundantly.

_____
_____
_____
_____
_____
_____

LESSON 1:
UNDERSTANDING LIGHT VS. DARK: WHAT IS LIGHT?

What does this imply about the paths in the world that we walk? Why is this so significant for us?

> **Read Proverbs 2:13:**
>
> ¹³ who forsake the paths of uprightness
>   to walk in the ways of darkness,

_____
_____
_____
_____

> **Read Proverbs 4:19:**
>
> ¹⁹ The way of the wicked is like deep darkness;
>   they do not know over what they stumble.

_____
_____
_____
_____
_____

What do these verses tell us about the difference between the wisdom of the world and the wisdom from God. What does this then imply about the world? Why is this so important for us to understand?

> **Read James 3:13–18:**
>
> Wisdom from Above
> ¹³ Who is wise and understanding among you? By his good conduct let him show his works in the meekness of wisdom. ¹⁴ But if you have bitter jealousy

LESSON 1:
UNDERSTANDING LIGHT VS. DARK: WHAT IS LIGHT?

> and selfish ambition in your hearts, do not boast and be false to the truth. [15] This is not the wisdom that comes down from above, but is earthly, unspiritual, demonic. [16] For where jealousy and selfish ambition exist, there will be disorder and every vile practice. [17] But the wisdom from above is first pure, then peaceable, gentle, open to reason, full of mercy and good fruits, impartial and sincere. [18] And a harvest of righteousness is sown in peace by those who make peace.

_____
_____
_____
_____
_____

Second: What is the significance of "light?"
It is the only way to the promised abundant life.
What does this say about the primary characteristic of light? Why is this so important to our life?

> **Read Ecclesiastes 2:13:**
>
> [13] Then I saw that there is more gain in wisdom than in folly, as there is more gain in light than in darkness.

_____
_____
_____
_____
_____

LESSON 1:
UNDERSTANDING LIGHT VS. DARK: WHAT IS LIGHT?

How does John describe the light? What is the power over darkness? What does this mean in our lives?

> **Read John 1:1–9:**
>
> The Word Became Flesh
> **1** In the beginning was the Word, and the Word was with God, and the Word was God. ² He was in the beginning with God. ³ All things were made through him, and without him was not any thing made that was made. ⁴ In him was
>
> life,[a] and the life was the light of men. ⁵ The light shines in the darkness, and the darkness has not overcome it.
> ⁶ There was a man sent from God, whose name was John. ⁷ He came as a witness, to bear witness about the light, that all might believe through him. ⁸ He was not the light, but came to bear witness about the light.
> ⁹ The true light, which gives light to everyone, was coming into the world.

_____
_____
_____
_____

What does Christ, the Light, promise those of us who follow Him? What does this mean about how we will experience life with Him?

> **Read John 10:10:**
>
> ¹⁰ The thief comes only to steal and kill and destroy. I came that they may have life and have it abundantly.

_____
_____
_____
_____
_____

LESSON 1:
UNDERSTANDING LIGHT VS. DARK: WHAT IS LIGHT?

1. What is "light?"

How does Christ describe Himself? What does this mean, and why is this important to our lives?

> **Read John 8:12:**
>
> I Am the Light of the World
> [12] Again Jesus spoke to them, saying, "I am the light of the world. Whoever follows me will not walk in darkness, but will have the light of life."

_____
_____
_____
_____
_____

Christ is the light – "I AM the Light of Life!"

In these verses, what are some of the characteristics of light? How will they be impactful in our everyday lives?

> **Read Daniel 5:11–12:**
>
> [11] There is a man in your kingdom in whom is the spirit of the holy gods.[a] In the days of your father, light and understanding and wisdom like the wisdom of the gods were found in him, and King Nebuchadnezzar, your father—your father the king—made him chief of the magicians, enchanters, Chaldeans, and astrologers,[12] because an excellent spirit, knowledge, and understanding to interpret dreams, explain riddles, and solve problems were found in this Daniel, whom the king named Belteshazzar. Now let Daniel be called, and he will show the interpretation."

_____
_____
_____
_____
_____

LESSON 1:
UNDERSTANDING LIGHT VS. DARK: WHAT IS LIGHT?

In order for us to experience the light, what is necessary that we understand about the light? How do we live this out so that we receive the power of the light?

> **Read 1 Timothy 6:13–16:**
>
> [13] I charge you in the presence of God, who gives life to all things, and of Christ Jesus, who in his testimony before[a] Pontius Pilate made the good confession, [14] to keep the commandment unstained and free from reproach until the appearing of our Lord Jesus Christ, [15] which he will display at the proper time—he who is the blessed and only Sovereign, the King of kings and Lord of lords, [16] who alone has immortality, who dwells in unapproachable light, whom no one has ever seen or can see. To him be honor and eternal dominion. Amen.

_____
_____
_____
_____
_____

In this story of Jesus appearing before Pilate, what did Paul want us to understand about Christ being King of kings? What did Jesus say that was so important that we need to receive? What does this look like in our everyday lives?

> **Read John 18:18–38:**
>
> [18] Now the servants[a] and officers had made a charcoal fire, because it was cold, and they were standing and warming themselves. Peter also was with them, standing and warming himself.
>
> The High Priest Questions Jesus
> [19] The high priest then questioned Jesus about his disciples and his teaching. [20] Jesus answered him, "I have spoken openly to the world. I have always taught in synagogues and in the temple, where all Jews come together. I have said nothing in secret. [21] Why do you ask me? Ask those who have heard me what I said to them; they know what I said." [22] When he had said these things, one of the officers standing by struck Jesus with his hand, saying, "Is that how you answer the high priest?" [23] Jesus answered him, "If what I said is wrong,

LESSON 1:
UNDERSTANDING LIGHT VS. DARK: WHAT IS LIGHT?

bear witness about the wrong; but if what I said is right, why do you strike me?" 24 Annas then sent him bound to Caiaphas the high priest.

Peter Denies Jesus Again
25 Now Simon Peter was standing and warming himself. So they said to him, "You also are not one of his disciples, are you?" He denied it and said, "I am not." 26 One of the servants of the high priest, a relative of the man whose ear Peter had cut off, asked, "Did I not see you in the garden with him?" 27 Peter again denied it, and at once a rooster crowed.

Jesus Before Pilate
28 Then they led Jesus from the house of Caiaphas to the governor's headquarters.[b] It was early morning. They themselves did not enter the governor's headquarters, so that they would not be defiled, but could eat the Passover. 29 So Pilate went outside to them and said, "What accusation do you bring against this man?" 30 They answered him, "If this man were not doing evil, we would not have delivered him over to you." 31 Pilate said to them, "Take him yourselves and judge him by your own law." The Jews said to him, "It is not lawful for us to put anyone to death." 32 This was to fulfill the word that Jesus had spoken to show by what kind of death he was going to die.

My Kingdom Is Not of This World
33 So Pilate entered his headquarters again and called Jesus and said to him, "Are you the King of the Jews?" 34 Jesus answered, "Do you say this of your own accord, or did others say it to you about me?" 35 Pilate answered, "Am I a Jew? Your own nation and the chief priests have delivered you over to me. What have you done?" 36 Jesus answered, "My kingdom is not of this world. If my kingdom were of this world, my servants would have been fighting, that I might not be delivered over to the Jews. But my kingdom is not from the world." 37 Then Pilate said to him, "So you are a king?" Jesus answered, "You say that I am a king. For this purpose I was born and for this purpose I have come into the world—to bear witness to the truth. Everyone who is of the truth listens to my voice." 38 Pilate said to him, "What is truth?"

After he had said this, he went back outside to the Jews and told them, "I find no guilt in him.

LESSON 1:
UNDERSTANDING LIGHT VS. DARK: WHAT IS LIGHT?

_____
_____
_____
_____

What does this tell us about light and dark? How important is this to how we live? What exactly does this practically mean in our everyday lives?

> **Read 2 Corinthians 6:14–18:**
>
> The Temple of the Living God
> 14 Do not be unequally yoked with unbelievers. For what partnership has righteousness with lawlessness? Or what fellowship has light with darkness? 15 What accord has Christ with Belial?[a] Or what portion does a believer share with an unbeliever? 16 What agreement has the temple of God with idols? For we are the temple of the living God; as God said,
> "I will make my dwelling among them and walk among them,
>   and I will be their God,
>   and they shall be my people.
> 17 Therefore go out from their midst,
>   and be separate from them, says the Lord,
> and touch no unclean thing;
>   then I will welcome you,
> 18 and I will be a father to you,
>   and you shall be sons and daughters to me,
> says the Lord Almighty."

_____
_____
_____
_____

LESSON 1:
UNDERSTANDING LIGHT VS. DARK: WHAT IS LIGHT?

What do these verses (which we do understand about the wonderful work of Christ for us) say about the difference between evil and light? Thus, what is the key for us to pursue in all aspects of our lives? What does that look like?

> **Read John 3:16–21:**
>
> For God So Loved the World
> 16 "For God so loved the world,[a] that he gave his only Son, that whoever believes in him should not perish but have eternal life. 17 For God did not send his Son into the world to condemn the world, but in order that the world might be saved through him. 18 Whoever believes in him is not condemned, but whoever does not believe is condemned already, because he has not believed in the name of the only Son of God. 19 And this is the judgment: the light has come into the world, and people loved the darkness rather than the light because their works were evil. 20 For everyone who does wicked things hates the light and does not come to the light, lest his works should be exposed. 21 But whoever does what is true comes to the light, so that it may be clearly seen that his works have been carried out in God."

_____
_____
_____
_____
_____

LESSON 2:
WHAT DOES THE "LIGHT" PROVIDE? WHAT IS OUR ROLE?

What does the "Light" provide for His children?

What does the Light lead us to? What happens there, and why is that so beneficial to us?

> **Read Psalm 43:3–4:**
>
> ³ Send out your light and your truth;
>   let them lead me;
> let them bring me to your holy hill
>   and to your dwelling!
> ⁴ Then I will go to the altar of God,
>   to God my exceeding joy,
> and I will praise you with the lyre,
>   O God, my God.

> "One of the highest priorities of the light is to bring us to truth."

_____
_____
_____
_____
_____
_____

LESSON 2:
WHAT DOES THE "LIGHT" PROVIDE? WHAT IS OUR ROLE?

What do these verses promise are the benefits of walking in the light? Why are they so meaningful to us and our lives?

> **Read Psalm 4:6–8:**
>
> [6] There are many who say, "Who will show us some good?
>   Lift up the light of your face upon us, O Lord!"
> [7] You have put more joy in my heart
>   than they have when their grain and wine abound.
> [8] In peace I will both lie down and sleep;
>   for you alone, O Lord, make me dwell in safety.

_____
_____
_____
_____
_____

What are the benefits of walking in the light? What do these mean to us practically?

> **Read Ephesians 5:8–9:**
>
> [8] for at one time you were darkness, but now you are light in the Lord. Walk as children of light [9] (for the fruit of light is found in all that is good and right and true),

_____
_____
_____
_____
_____

LESSON 2:
WHAT DOES THE "LIGHT" PROVIDE?
WHAT IS OUR ROLE?

What does this story relate about a profound truth about the light? How does this impact our life and how we approach living in the light?

> **Read Luke 8:16–18:**
>
> A Lamp Under a Jar
> [16] "No one after lighting a lamp covers it with a jar or puts it under a bed, but puts it on a stand, so that those who enter may see the light. [17] For nothing is hidden that will not be made manifest, nor is anything secret that will not be known and come to light. [18] Take care then how you hear, for to the one who has, more will be given, and from the one who has not, even what he thinks that he has will be taken away."

_____
_____
_____
_____

What are the benefits of walking in the light? What do these mean to our lives?

> **Read Isaiah 58:6–12:**
>
> [6] "Is not this the fast that I choose:
>   to loose the bonds of wickedness,
> to undo the straps of the yoke,
> to let the oppressed[a] go free,
>   and to break every yoke?
> [7] Is it not to share your bread with the hungry
>   and bring the homeless poor into your house;
> when you see the naked, to cover him,
>   and not to hide yourself from your own flesh?
> [8] Then shall your light break forth like the dawn,
>   and your healing shall spring up speedily;
> your righteousness shall go before you;
>   the glory of the Lord shall be your rear guard.
> [9] Then you shall call, and the Lord will answer;
>   you shall cry, and he will say, 'Here I am.'
> If you take away the yoke from your midst,

LESSON 2:
WHAT DOES THE "LIGHT" PROVIDE? WHAT IS OUR ROLE?

> the pointing of the finger, and speaking wickedness,
> ¹⁰ if you pour yourself out for the hungry
>   and satisfy the desire of the afflicted,
> then shall your light rise in the darkness
>   and your gloom be as the noonday.
> ¹¹ And the Lord will guide you continually
>   and satisfy your desire in scorched places
>   and make your bones strong;
> and you shall be like a watered garden,
>   like a spring of water,
>   whose waters do not fail.
> ¹² And your ancient ruins shall be rebuilt;
>   you shall raise up the foundations of many generations;
> you shall be called the repairer of the breach,
>   the restorer of streets to dwell in.

_____
_____
_____
_____
_____

As you live in the light, what do you become? Why is that a wonderful benefit to you and to others? What does that look like in your life?

> **Read Isaiah 42:6–9:**
>
> ⁶ "I am the Lord; I have called you[a] in righteousness;
>   I will take you by the hand and keep you;
> I will give you as a covenant for the people,
>   a light for the nations,
> ⁷   to open the eyes that are blind,
> to bring out the prisoners from the dungeon,
>   from the prison those who sit in darkness.
> ⁸ I am the Lord; that is my name;
>   my glory I give to no other,

LESSON 2:
WHAT DOES THE "LIGHT" PROVIDE? WHAT IS OUR ROLE?

> nor my praise to carved idols.
> ⁹ Behold, the former things have come to pass,
>   and new things I now declare;
> before they spring forth
>   I tell you of them."

_____
_____
_____
_____
_____

What does Christ speak here about receiving things in private? Why is this important, and what benefit will we accrue?

> **Read Matthew 10:27–31:**
>
> ²⁷ What I tell you in the dark, say in the light, and what you hear whispered, proclaim on the housetops. ²⁸ And do not fear those who kill the body but cannot kill the soul. Rather fear him who can destroy both soul and body in hell.[a] ²⁹ Are not two sparrows sold for a penny?[b] And not one of them will fall to the ground apart from your Father. ³⁰ But even the hairs of your head are all numbered. ³¹ Fear not, therefore; you are of more value than many sparrows.

_____
_____
_____
_____
_____
_____

LESSON 2:
WHAT DOES THE "LIGHT" PROVIDE? WHAT IS OUR ROLE?

Our role is very clear and necessary to experience benefits.

Key principles:

What does it mean to "work out your own salvation"? How do we do that, and how does it relate to following God and living in the light? What practically does that mean to us?

> **Read Philippians 2:12–15:**
>
> Lights in the World
> 12 Therefore, my beloved, as you have always obeyed, so now, not only as in my presence but much more in my absence, work out your own salvation with fear and trembling, 13 for it is God who works in you, both to will and to work for his good pleasure.
>
> 14 Do all things without grumbling or disputing, 15 that you may be blameless and innocent, children of God without blemish in the midst of a crooked and twisted generation, among whom you shine as lights in the world,

_____
_____
_____
_____

With this description of the oil and the lamp, what is the spiritual principle that is important for us to understand? What does that mean for each of us personally?

> **Read Exodus 27:20–21; 35:4–9, 27–29:**
>
> Oil for the Lamp
> 20 "You shall command the people of Israel that they bring to you pure beaten olive oil for the light, that a lamp may regularly be set up to burn. 21 In the tent of meeting, outside the veil that is before the testimony, Aaron and his sons shall tend it from evening to morning before the Lord. It shall be a statute forever to be observed throughout their generations by the people of Israel.

LESSON 2:
WHAT DOES THE "LIGHT" PROVIDE?
WHAT IS OUR ROLE?

> Contributions for the Tabernacle
>
> 4 Moses said to all the congregation of the people of Israel, "This is the thing that the Lord has commanded. 5 Take from among you a contribution to the Lord. Whoever is of a generous heart, let him bring the Lord's contribution: gold, silver, and bronze; 6 blue and purple and scarlet yarns and fine twined linen; goats' hair, 7 tanned rams' skins, and goatskins;[a] acacia wood, 8 oil for the light, spices for the anointing oil and for the fragrant incense, 9 and onyx stones and stones for setting, for the ephod and for the breastpiece.
>
> 27 And the leaders brought onyx stones and stones to be set, for the ephod and for the breastpiece, 28 and spices and oil for the light, and for the anointing oil, and for the fragrant incense. 29 All the men and women, the people of Israel, whose heart moved them to bring anything for the work that the Lord had commanded by Moses to be done brought it as a free will offering to the Lord.

_____
_____
_____
_____
_____

If we are walking in the light, who must we know, experience, and follow? Why is this important, particularly versus studying about the light? What is the difference, and what difference will it mean in our life?

> **Read John 1:6–9:**
>
> 6 There was a man sent from God, whose name was John. 7 He came as a witness, to bear witness about the light, that all might believe through him. 8 He was not the light, but came to bear witness about the light.
> 9 The true light, which gives light to everyone, was coming into the world.

_____
_____
_____
_____
_____

LESSON 2:
WHAT DOES THE "LIGHT" PROVIDE?
WHAT IS OUR ROLE?

What does John say about our role with the light, and what we are to pursue and enjoy? Why? What does this look like in our personal lives?

> **Read John 3:22–36:**
>
> John the Baptist Exalts Christ
>
> 22 After this Jesus and his disciples went into the Judean countryside, and he remained there with them and was baptizing. 23 John also was baptizing at Aenon near Salim, because water was plentiful there, and people were coming and being baptized 24 (for John had not yet been put in prison).
>
> 25 Now a discussion arose between some of John's disciples and a Jew over purification. 26 And they came to John and said to him, "Rabbi, he who was with you across the Jordan, to whom you bore witness—look, he is baptizing, and all are going to him." 27 John answered, "A person cannot receive even one thing unless it is given him from heaven. 28 You yourselves bear me witness, that I said, 'I am not the Christ, but I have been sent before him.' 29 The one who has the bride is the bridegroom. The friend of the bridegroom, who stands and hears him, rejoices greatly at the bridegroom's voice. Therefore this joy of mine is now complete. 30 He must increase, but I must decrease."[a]
>
> 31 He who comes from above is above all. He who is of the earth belongs to the earth and speaks in an earthly way. He who comes from heaven is above all. 32 He bears witness to what he has seen and heard, yet no one receives his testimony. 33 Whoever receives his testimony sets his seal to this, that God is true. 34 For he whom God has sent utters the words of God, for he gives the Spirit without measure. 35 The Father loves the Son and has given all things into his hand. 36 Whoever believes in the Son has eternal life; whoever does not obey the Son shall not see life, but the wrath of God remains on him.

_____
_____
_____
_____
_____

LESSON 3:
WHAT IS OUR ROLE (CONTINUED)?

Our role is very clear and necessary to experience benefits.

Delight in Him – Abide:

What does it mean to delight in Him? As we do delight in Him, what does He promise? What does that mean to us personally?

> **Read Psalm 37:1–8:**
>
> He Will Not Forsake His Saints
> [a] Of David.
> **37** Fret not yourself because of evildoers;
>   be not envious of wrongdoers!
> ² For they will soon fade like the grass
>   and wither like the green herb.
> ³ Trust in the Lord, and do good;
>   dwell in the land and befriend faithfulness.[b]
> ⁴ Delight yourself in the Lord,
>   and he will give you the desires of your heart.
> ⁵ Commit your way to the Lord;
>   trust in him, and he will act.
> ⁶ He will bring forth your righteousness as the light,
>   and your justice as the noonday.
> ⁷ Be still before the Lord and wait patiently for him;
>   fret not yourself over the one who prospers in his way,
>   over the man who carries out evil devices!
> ⁸ Refrain from anger, and forsake wrath!
>   Fret not yourself; it tends only to evil.

> "It's not you taking charge. It's not you saying I'm going to make it happen. He will bring it to pass as you commit the pathway to Him..."

_____
_____
_____
_____
_____
_____

LESSON 3:
WHAT IS OUR ROLE (CONTINUED)?

What has Christ done regarding how we are placed in the light? What does that mean, and what is important for us to follow if we are to experience this? On what basis will we experience this?

> **Read Colossians 1:9–18:**
>
> 9 And so, from the day we heard, we have not ceased to pray for you, asking that you may be filled with the knowledge of his will in all spiritual wisdom and understanding, 10 so as to walk in a manner worthy of the Lord, fully pleasing to him: bearing fruit in every good work and increasing in the knowledge of God; 11 being strengthened with all power, according to his glorious might, for all endurance and patience with joy; 12 giving thanks[a] to the Father, who has qualified you[b] to share in the inheritance of the saints in light. 13 He has delivered us from the domain of darkness and transferred us to the kingdom of his beloved Son, 14 in whom we have redemption, the forgiveness of sins.
>
> The Preeminence of Christ
> 15 He is the image of the invisible God, the firstborn of all creation. 16 For by[c] him all things were created, in heaven and on earth, visible and invisible, whether thrones or dominions or rulers or authorities—all things were created through him and for him. 17 And he is before all things, and in him all things hold together. 18 And he is the head of the body, the church. He is the beginning, the firstborn from the dead, that in everything he might be preeminent.

_____
_____
_____
_____
_____

    All things were created by Him, and for Him. Thus, the material is subordinate to the spiritual.
    This world was created by Him speaking it (called Ex-nihilo) out of nothing. The material, the physical, all things literally were created by Him and for Him through Him speaking; this is the spiritual. He is above all things, because He is superior to all things. And there's nothing that is beyond His ability to influence, create

LESSON 3:
WHAT IS OUR ROLE (CONTINUED)?

Why is it critical for us to stay in the light? Why is this important for our heart, and what is the benefit of this to our lives?

> **Read Proverbs 4:18–23:**
>
> 18 But the path of the righteous is like the light of dawn,
>   which shines brighter and brighter until full day.
> 19 The way of the wicked is like deep darkness;
>   they do not know over what they stumble.
> 20 My son, be attentive to my words;
>   incline your ear to my sayings.
> 21 Let them not escape from your sight;
>   keep them within your heart.
> 22 For they are life to those who find them,
>   and healing to all their[a] flesh.
> 23 Keep your heart with all vigilance,
>   for from it flow the springs of life.

_____
_____
_____
_____
_____

LESSON 3:
WHAT IS OUR ROLE (CONTINUED)?

What do these stories tell us about the importance of experiencing living in the light? What does that mean for us, and what must be true for us?

> **Read Mark 4:21–25 and Luke 8:16–18:**
>
> A Lamp Under a Basket
> [21] And he said to them, "Is a lamp brought in to be put under a basket, or under a bed, and not on a stand? [22] For nothing is hidden except to be made manifest; nor is anything secret except to come to light. [23] If anyone has ears to hear, let him hear." [24] And he said to them, "Pay attention to what you hear: with the measure you use, it will be measured to you, and still more will be added to you. [25] For to the one who has, more will be given, and from the one who has not, even what he has will be taken away."
>
> A Lamp Under a Jar
> [16] "No one after lighting a lamp covers it with a jar or puts it under a bed, but puts it on a stand, so that those who enter may see the light. [17] For nothing is hidden that will not be made manifest, nor is anything secret that will not be known and come to light. [18] Take care then how you hear, for to the one who has, more will be given, and from the one who has not, even what he thinks that he has will be taken away."

_____
_____
_____
_____

LESSON 3:
WHAT IS OUR ROLE (CONTINUED)?

Word Definitions: What does Paul tell Timothy is a key characteristic for living in the light? What does this mean, and how do we live this out in our spiritual lives?

> **Read 1 Timothy 6:11–16:**
>
> Fight the Good Fight of Faith
> [11] But as for you, O man of God, flee these things. Pursue righteousness, godliness, faith, love, steadfastness, gentleness. [12] Fight the good fight of the faith. Take hold of the eternal life to which you were called and about which you made the good confession in the presence of many witnesses. [13] I charge you in the presence of God, who gives life to all things, and of Christ Jesus, who in his testimony before[a] Pontius Pilate made the good confession, [14] to keep the commandment unstained and free from reproach until the appearing of our Lord Jesus Christ, [15] which he will display at the proper time—he who is the blessed and only Sovereign, the King of kings and Lord of lords, [16] who alone has immortality, who dwells in unapproachable light, whom no one has ever seen or can see. To him be honor and eternal dominion. Amen.

_____
_____
_____
_____
_____

LESSON 3:
WHAT IS OUR ROLE (CONTINUED)?

What do each of these verses in Psalm 119 tell us about light and following the light? What are the benefits of doing so?

> **Read Psalm 119:105–106:**
>
> [105] Your word is a lamp to my feet
>   and a light to my path.
> [106] I have sworn an oath and confirmed it,
>   to keep your righteous rules.

_____
_____
_____
_____

> **Read Psalm 119:1–3:**
>
> Your Word Is a Lamp to My Feet
> Aleph
> **119** [a] Blessed are those whose way is blameless,
>   who walk in the law of the Lord!
> [2] Blessed are those who keep his testimonies,
>   who seek him with their whole heart,
> [3] who also do no wrong,
>   but walk in his ways!

_____
_____
_____
_____
_____

LESSON 3:
WHAT IS OUR ROLE (CONTINUED)?

Read Psalm 119:16–18:

¹⁶ I will delight in your statutes;
    I will not forget your word.

Gimel
¹⁷ Deal bountifully with your servant,
  that I may live and keep your word.
¹⁸ Open my eyes, that I may behold
  wondrous things out of your law.

_____
_____
_____
_____
_____

Read Psalm 119:33–35:

He
³³ Teach me, O Lord, the way of your statutes;
  and I will keep it to the end.[a]
³⁴ Give me understanding, that I may keep your law
  and observe it with my whole heart.
³⁵ Lead me in the path of your commandments,
  for I delight in it.

_____
_____
_____
_____
_____

LESSON 3:
WHAT IS OUR ROLE (CONTINUED)?

> **Read Psalm 119:97–100:**
>
> Mem
> 97 Oh how I love your law!
>   It is my meditation all the day.
> 98 Your commandment makes me wiser than my enemies,
>   for it is ever with me.
> 99 I have more understanding than all my teachers,
>   for your testimonies are my meditation.
> 100 I understand more than the aged,[a]
>   for I keep your precepts.

_____
_____
_____
_____

> **Read Psalm 119:129–130:**
>
> Pe
> 129 Your testimonies are wonderful;
>   therefore my soul keeps them.
> 130 The unfolding of your words gives light;
>   it imparts understanding to the simple.

_____
_____
_____
_____

LESSON 3:
WHAT IS OUR ROLE (CONTINUED)?

Walk in the Light:

What does this speak to about what is important to walking in the light? Why? What does that mean as we consider our life right now as we are to walk in light?

> **Read Ephesians 5:8–14:**
>
> 8 for at one time you were darkness, but now you are light in the Lord. Walk as children of light 9 (for the fruit of light is found in all that is good and right and true), 10 and try to discern what is pleasing to the Lord. 11 Take no part in the unfruitful works of darkness, but instead expose them. 12 For it is shameful even to speak of the things that they do in secret. 13 But when anything is exposed by the light, it becomes visible, 14 for anything that becomes visible is light. Therefore it says,
> "Awake, O sleeper,
> and arise from the dead,
> and Christ will shine on you."

_____
_____
_____
_____

To walk in the light, what is Christ's simple instruction to us? What does this truly mean, and how do we carry this out?

> **Read John 8:12:**
>
> I Am the Light of the World
> 12 Again Jesus spoke to them, saying, "I am the light of the world. Whoever follows me will not walk in darkness, but will have the light of life."

LESSON 3:
WHAT IS OUR ROLE (CONTINUED)?

_____
_____
_____
_____
_____

What is the key to being led to freedom? What does this mean in our lives, and how do we carry this out practically?

> **Read John 8:31–32:**
>
> The Truth Will Set You Free
> [31] So Jesus said to the Jews who had believed him, "If you abide in my word, you are truly my disciples, [32] and you will know the truth, and the truth will set you free."

_____
_____
_____
_____

LESSON 3:
WHAT IS OUR ROLE (CONTINUED)?

What do these verses tell us about our role in living in light versus dark. Why is this so important, and how do we carry this out?

Read 2 Corinthians 6:11–18:

[11] We have spoken freely to you,[a] Corinthians; our heart is wide open. [12] You are not restricted by us, but you are restricted in your own affections. [13] In return (I speak as to children) widen your hearts also.

The Temple of the Living God
[14] Do not be unequally yoked with unbelievers. For what partnership has righteousness with lawlessness? Or what fellowship has light with darkness? [15] What accord has Christ with Belial?[b] Or what portion does a believer share with an unbeliever? [16] What agreement has the temple of God with idols? For we are the temple of the living God; as God said,
"I will make my dwelling among them and walk among them,
 and I will be their God,
 and they shall be my people.
[17] Therefore go out from their midst,
 and be separate from them, says the Lord,
and touch no unclean thing;
 then I will welcome you,
[18] and I will be a father to you,
 and you shall be sons and daughters to me,
says the Lord Almighty."

_____
_____
_____
_____
_____

LESSON 3:
WHAT IS OUR ROLE (CONTINUED)?

What do these verses say about the key to staying in the light? What is critical for how we walk with God? How does this play out in our everyday life?

> **Read Isaiah 5:20–21:**
>
> ²⁰ Woe to those who call evil good
>   and good evil,
> who put darkness for light
>   and light for darkness,
> who put bitter for sweet
>   and sweet for bitter!
> ²¹ Woe to those who are wise in their own eyes,
>   and shrewd in their own sight!

_____
_____
_____
_____
_____

LESSON 4:
WHAT IS OUR ROLE? (CONTINUED)

Walk in the Light (Continued):

What do these verses say about the importance of what we look at and what we serve ? What does this mean to us, and how do we fulfill this in our everyday lives?

> **Read Matthew 6:22–24:**
>
> 22 "The eye is the lamp of the body. So, if your eye is healthy, your whole body will be full of light, 23 but if your eye is bad, your whole body will be full of darkness. If then the light in you is darkness, how great is the darkness!
>
> 24 "No one can serve two masters, for either he will hate the one and love the other, or he will be devoted to the one and despise the other. You cannot serve God and money.[a]

> "The key is to go to God with a surrendered heart—serve Him, and ask Him to guide us to resolve what we are looking at, what decisions to make, etc."

_____
_____
_____
_____
_____

LESSON 4:
WHAT IS OUR ROLE? (CONTINUED)

What does Jesus say here about what to beware of? Why? What does this mean about how we live out our lives?

> **Read Mark 8:14–20:**
>
> The Leaven of the Pharisees and Herod
> 14 Now they had forgotten to bring bread, and they had only one loaf with them in the boat. 15 And he cautioned them, saying, "Watch out; beware of the leaven of the Pharisees and the leaven of Herod."[a] 16 And they began discussing with one another the fact that they had no bread. 17 And Jesus, aware of this, said to them, "Why are you discussing the fact that you have no bread? Do you not yet perceive or understand? Are your hearts hardened? 18 Having eyes do you not see, and having ears do you not hear? And do you not remember? 19 When I broke the five loaves for the five thousand, how many baskets full of broken pieces did you take up?" They said to him, "Twelve." 20 "And the seven for the four thousand, how many baskets full of broken pieces did you take up?" And they said to him, "Seven."

_____
_____
_____
_____

As we walk in the light, what are we to be careful of? What does that mean, and how do we apply this to our lives?

> **Read 2 Corinthians 11:12–15:**
>
> 12 And what I am doing I will continue to do, in order to undermine the claim of those who would like to claim that in their boasted mission they work on the same terms as we do. 13 For such men are false apostles, deceitful workmen, disguising themselves as apostles of Christ. 14 And no wonder, for even Satan disguises himself as an angel of light. 15 So it is no surprise if his servants, also, disguise themselves as servants of righteousness. Their end will correspond to their deeds.

LESSON 4:
WHAT IS OUR ROLE? (CONTINUED)

_____
_____
_____
_____
_____

What does God say about the snare of riches? How are we to reconcile this with the necessity of provision and finances? What does this mean to us practically?

> **Read 1 Timothy 6:6–11:**
>
> [6] But godliness with contentment is great gain, [7] for we brought nothing into the world, and[a] we cannot take anything out of the world. [8] But if we have food and clothing, with these we will be content. [9] But those who desire to be rich fall into temptation, into a snare, into many senseless and harmful desires that plunge people into ruin and destruction. [10] For the love of money is a root of all kinds of evils. It is through this craving that some have wandered away from the faith and pierced themselves with many pangs.
>
> **Fight the Good Fight of Faith**
> [11] But as for you, O man of God, flee these things. Pursue righteousness, godliness, faith, love, steadfastness, gentleness.

_____
_____
_____
_____
_____

LESSON 4:
WHAT IS OUR ROLE? (CONTINUED)

What does Jesus say about what happens when you walk in darkness? Why is that important to us? What is His admonition about the light? What does that mean, and how do we live this out?

> **Read John 12:27–36:**
>
> The Son of Man Must Be Lifted Up
> [27] "Now is my soul troubled. And what shall I say? 'Father, save me from this hour'? But for this purpose I have come to this hour. [28] Father, glorify your name." Then a voice came from heaven: "I have glorified it, and I will glorify it again." [29] The crowd that stood there and heard it said that it had thundered. Others said, "An angel has spoken to him." [30] Jesus answered, "This voice has come for your sake, not mine. [31] Now is the judgment of this world; now will the ruler of this world be cast out. [32] And I, when I am lifted up from the earth, will draw all people to myself." [33] He said this to show by what kind of death he was going to die. [34] So the crowd answered him, "We have heard from the Law that the Christ remains forever. How can you say that the Son of Man must be lifted up? Who is this Son of Man?" [35] So Jesus said to them, "The light is among you for a little while longer. Walk while you have the light, lest darkness overtake you. The one who walks in the darkness does not know where he is going. [36] While you have the light, believe in the light, that you may become sons of light."
>
> The Unbelief of the People
> When Jesus had said these things, he departed and hid himself from them.

_____
_____
_____
_____
_____

LESSON 4:
WHAT IS OUR ROLE? (CONTINUED)

Read John 12:42–50:

42 Nevertheless, many even of the authorities believed in him, but for fear of the Pharisees they did not confess it, so that they would not be put out of the synagogue; 43 for they loved the glory that comes from man more than the glory that comes from God.

Jesus Came to Save the World
44 And Jesus cried out and said, "Whoever believes in me, believes not in me but in him who sent me. 45 And whoever sees me sees him who sent me. 46 I have come into the world as light, so that whoever believes in me may not remain in darkness. 47 If anyone hears my words and does not keep them, I do not judge him; for I did not come to judge the world but to save the world. 48 The one who rejects me and does not receive my words has a judge; the word that I have spoken will judge him on the last day. 49 For I have not spoken on my own authority, but the Father who sent me has himself given me a commandment—what to say and what to speak. 50 And I know that his commandment is eternal life. What I say, therefore, I say as the Father has told me."

_____
_____
_____
_____
_____

LESSON 4:
WHAT IS OUR ROLE? (CONTINUED)

Call on the Lord for everything:
When we are having difficulty or trouble, what are we to do? Why? How do we live this out practically in our lives?

> **Read Psalm 27:1–4:**
>
> The Lord Is My Light and My Salvation
> Of David.
> **27** The Lord is my light and my salvation;
>   whom shall I fear?
> The Lord is the stronghold[a] of my life;
>   of whom shall I be afraid?
> ² When evildoers assail me
>   to eat up my flesh,
> my adversaries and foes,
>   it is they who stumble and fall.
> ³ Though an army encamp against me,
>   my heart shall not fear;
> though war arise against me,
>   yet[b] I will be confident.
> ⁴ One thing have I asked of the Lord,
>   that will I seek after:
> that I may dwell in the house of the Lord
>   all the days of my life,
> to gaze upon the beauty of the Lord
>   and to inquire[c] in his temple.

_____
_____
_____
_____
_____

LESSON 4:
WHAT IS OUR ROLE? (CONTINUED)

Read Psalm 27:13–14:

13 I believe that I shall look[a] upon the goodness of the Lord
   in the land of the living!
14 Wait for the Lord;
   be strong, and let your heart take courage;
   wait for the Lord!

_____
_____
_____
_____
_____

In these two sets of verses in Psalm 18, what does He say to us about what to do when we are in great difficulty, in great trouble? Why is this so important? What does this mean regarding how we approach the issues of life?

Read Psalm 18:1–6:

The Lord Is My Rock and My Fortress
To the choirmaster. A Psalm of David, the servant of the Lord, who addressed the words of this song to the Lord on the day when the Lord delivered him from the hand of all his enemies, and from the hand of Saul. He said:

18 I love you, O Lord, my strength.
² The Lord is my rock and my fortress and my deliverer,
   my God, my rock, in whom I take refuge,
   my shield, and the horn of my salvation, my stronghold.
³ I call upon the Lord, who is worthy to be praised,
   and I am saved from my enemies.
⁴ The cords of death encompassed me;
   the torrents of destruction assailed me;[a]
⁵ the cords of Sheol entangled me;
   the snares of death confronted me.

LESSON 4:
WHAT IS OUR ROLE? (CONTINUED)

> ⁶ In my distress I called upon the Lord;
>   to my God I cried for help.
> From his temple he heard my voice,
>   and my cry to him reached his ears.

_____
_____
_____
_____

Read Psalm 18:25–28:

> ²⁵ With the merciful you show yourself merciful;
>   with the blameless man you show yourself blameless;
> ²⁶ with the purified you show yourself pure;
>   and with the crooked you make yourself seem tortuous.
> ²⁷ For you save a humble people,
>   but the haughty eyes you bring down.
> ²⁸ For it is you who light my lamp;
>   the Lord my God lightens my darkness.

_____
_____
_____
_____

LESSON 4:
WHAT IS OUR ROLE? (CONTINUED)

Do not judge, including judgement of self:
What does Paul tell us about judging, including ourselves? Why is this so important to learn? How do we apply this in our situations?

> **Read 1 Corinthians 4:1–5:**
>
> The Ministry of Apostles
> **4** This is how one should regard us, as servants of Christ and stewards of the mysteries of God. ² Moreover, it is required of stewards that they be found faithful. ³ But with me it is a very small thing that I should be judged by you or by any human court. In fact, I do not even judge myself. ⁴ For I am not aware of anything against myself, but I am not thereby acquitted. It is the Lord who judges me. ⁵ Therefore do not pronounce judgment before the time, before the Lord comes, who will bring to light the things now hidden in darkness and will disclose the purposes of the heart. Then each one will receive his commendation from God.

_____
_____
_____
_____
_____

What does Paul say about the importance of watching for things that happen in the end times? What does this mean for us in the times we live in, and how do we thus approach the times we live in?

> **Read 1 Thessalonians 5:1–11:**
>
> The Day of the Lord
> **5** Now concerning the times and the seasons, brothers,[a] you have no need to have anything written to you. ² For you yourselves are fully aware that the day of the Lord will come like a thief in the night. ³ While people are saying, "There is peace and security," then sudden destruction will come upon them as labor pains come upon a pregnant woman, and they will not escape. ⁴ But you are not in darkness, brothers, for that day to surprise you like a thief. ⁵ For you are all children[b] of light, children of the day. We are not of the night or of the darkness. ⁶ So then let us not sleep, as others do, but let us keep awake and be sober. ⁷ For those who sleep, sleep at night, and those who get drunk, are drunk

LESSON 4:
WHAT IS OUR ROLE? (CONTINUED)

> at night. 8 But since we belong to the day, let us be sober, having put on the breastplate of faith and love, and for a helmet the hope of salvation. 9 For God has not destined us for wrath, but to obtain salvation through our Lord Jesus Christ, 10 who died for us so that whether we are awake or asleep we might live with him. 11 Therefore encourage one another and build one another up, just as you are doing.

_____
_____
_____
_____

As we work out our own salvation (which we discussed above), what will be the outcome of walking in the light? What can we expect, and what then will motivate us to walk in the light?

> **Read Philippians 2:12–18:**
>
> Lights in the World
> 12 Therefore, my beloved, as you have always obeyed, so now, not only as in my presence but much more in my absence, work out your own salvation with fear and trembling, 13 for it is God who works in you, both to will and to work for his good pleasure.
>
> 14 Do all things without grumbling or disputing, 15 that you may be blameless and innocent, children of God without blemish in the midst of a crooked and twisted generation, among whom you shine as lights in the world, 16 holding fast to the word of life, so that in the day of Christ I may be proud that I did not run in vain or labor in vain. 17 Even if I am to be poured out as a drink offering upon the sacrificial offering of your faith, I am glad and rejoice with you all. 18 Likewise you also should be glad and rejoice with me.

_____
_____
_____
_____
_____

LESSON 5:
RESULTS OF "WALKING IN THE LIGHT" AND OUR CALL TO "GIVE IT AWAY"

What are the results of His children walking in the light?

What do these verses in Psalm 18 relate as the benefits of walking in the light? What do they practically mean to us in our lives?

Read Psalm 18:1–3:

The Lord Is My Rock and My Fortress
To the choirmaster. A Psalm of David, the servant of the Lord, who addressed the words of this song to the Lord on the day when the Lord delivered him from the hand of all his enemies, and from the hand of Saul. He said:

18 I love you, O Lord, my strength.
² The Lord is my rock and my fortress and my deliverer,
    my God, my rock, in whom I take refuge,
    my shield, and the horn of my salvation, my stronghold.
³ I call upon the Lord, who is worthy to be praised,
    and I am saved from my enemies.

> **"God is giving us the abundant life, the absolute exceptional life that He has planned for us, if we would allow Him to lead us into it, the enemy's not going to steal it from us."**

_____
_____
_____
_____
_____
_____
_____

LESSON 5:
RESULTS OF "WALKING IN THE LIGHT" AND OUR CALL TO "GIVE IT AWAY"

Read Psalm 18:16–19:

¹⁶ He sent from on high, he took me;
  he drew me out of many waters.
¹⁷ He rescued me from my strong enemy
  and from those who hated me,
  for they were too mighty for me.
¹⁸ They confronted me in the day of my calamity,
  but the Lord was my support.
¹⁹ He brought me out into a broad place;
  he rescued me, because he delighted in me.

_____
_____
_____
_____

Read Psalm 18:28–36:

²⁸ For it is you who light my lamp;
  the Lord my God lightens my darkness.
²⁹ For by you I can run against a troop,
  and by my God I can leap over a wall.
³⁰ This God—his way is perfect;[a]
  the word of the Lord proves true;
  he is a shield for all those who take refuge in him.
³¹ For who is God, but the Lord?
  And who is a rock, except our God?—
³² the God who equipped me with strength
  and made my way blameless.
³³ He made my feet like the feet of a deer
  and set me secure on the heights.
³⁴ He trains my hands for war,
  so that my arms can bend a bow of bronze.
³⁵ You have given me the shield of your salvation,

LESSON 5:
RESULTS OF "WALKING IN THE LIGHT" AND OUR CALL TO "GIVE IT AWAY"

> and your right hand supported me,
>   and your gentleness made me great.
> ³⁶ You gave a wide place for my steps under me,
>   and my feet did not slip.

_____
_____
_____
_____
_____

As you walk in the light, what does God promise He will do with the obstacles in our way? How will He lead us on our path? What does that look like in our everyday lives?

> **Read Isaiah 45:1–6:**
>
> Cyrus, God's Instrument
> **45** Thus says the Lord to his anointed, to Cyrus,
>   whose right hand I have grasped,
> to subdue nations before him
>   and to loose the belts of kings,
> to open doors before him
>   that gates may not be closed:
> ² "I will go before you
>   and level the exalted places,[a]
> I will break in pieces the doors of bronze
>   and cut through the bars of iron,
> ³ I will give you the treasures of darkness
>   and the hoards in secret places,
> that you may know that it is I, the Lord,
>   the God of Israel, who call you by your name.
> ⁴ For the sake of my servant Jacob,
>   and Israel my chosen,
> I call you by your name,
>   I name you, though you do not know me.

LESSON 5:
RESULTS OF "WALKING IN THE LIGHT" AND OUR CALL TO "GIVE IT AWAY"

> ⁵ I am the Lord, and there is no other,
>   besides me there is no God;
>   I equip you, though you do not know me,
> ⁶ that people may know, from the rising of the sun
>   and from the west, that there is none besides me;
> I am the Lord, and there is no other.

_____
_____
_____
_____
_____

What is the amazing benefit of walking in the light? What does this imply to us that is broader than just financial? Why is this important to us?

Read Psalm 118:25–29:

> ²⁵ Save us, we pray, O Lord!
>   O Lord, we pray, give us success!
> ²⁶ Blessed is he who comes in the name of the Lord!
>   We bless you from the house of the Lord.
> ²⁷ The Lord is God,
>   and he has made his light to shine upon us.
> Bind the festal sacrifice with cords,
>   up to the horns of the altar!
> ²⁸ You are my God, and I will give thanks to you;
>   you are my God; I will extol you.
> ²⁹ Oh give thanks to the Lord, for he is good;
>   for his steadfast love endures forever!

_____
_____
_____
_____
_____

LESSON 5:
RESULTS OF "WALKING IN THE LIGHT" AND OUR CALL TO "GIVE IT AWAY"

As we walk on this path, what happens to us on this path? Why is that so interesting and so important for us? How do we stay on that path?

> **Read Proverbs 4:18–23:**
>
> 18 But the path of the righteous is like the light of dawn,
>   which shines brighter and brighter until full day.
> 19 The way of the wicked is like deep darkness;
>   they do not know over what they stumble.
> 20 My son, be attentive to my words;
>   incline your ear to my sayings.
> 21 Let them not escape from your sight;
>   keep them within your heart.
> 22 For they are life to those who find them,
>   and healing to all their[a] flesh.
> 23 Keep your heart with all vigilance,
>   for from it flow the springs of life.

_____
_____
_____
_____
_____

What does God promise as we walk in the light? What does that mean to us? What is required of us?

> **Read Psalm 37:1–8:**
>
> He Will Not Forsake His Saints
> [a] Of David.
> **37** Fret not yourself because of evildoers;
>   be not envious of wrongdoers!
> 2 For they will soon fade like the grass
>   and wither like the green herb.
> 3 Trust in the Lord, and do good;

LESSON 5:
RESULTS OF "WALKING IN THE LIGHT" AND OUR CALL TO "GIVE IT AWAY"

> dwell in the land and befriend faithfulness.[b]
>
> ⁴ Delight yourself in the Lord,
>   and he will give you the desires of your heart.
> ⁵ Commit your way to the Lord;
>   trust in him, and he will act.
> ⁶ He will bring forth your righteousness as the light,
>   and your justice as the noonday.
> ⁷ Be still before the Lord and wait patiently for him;
>   fret not yourself over the one who prospers in his way,
>   over the man who carries out evil devices!
> ⁸ Refrain from anger, and forsake wrath!
>   Fret not yourself; it tends only to evil.

_____
_____
_____
_____

Our call is to give it away—Covenant:

As part of the covenant, and as we walk in the light, what will we be asked to do? What will be our joy in being part of this, and why is this so important to God's bigger story?

> **Read Isaiah 60:1–3:**
>
> The Future Glory of Israel
>
> **60** Arise, shine, for your light has come,
>   and the glory of the Lord has risen upon you.
> ² For behold, darkness shall cover the earth,
>   and thick darkness the peoples;
> but the Lord will arise upon you,
>   and his glory will be seen upon you.
> ³ And nations shall come to your light,
>   and kings to the brightness of your rising.

LESSON 5:
RESULTS OF "WALKING IN THE LIGHT" AND OUR CALL TO "GIVE IT AWAY"

_____
_____
_____
_____
_____

What do these verses say we actually become? What does this mean regarding our assignments and how we give it away? How will we experience this?

> **Read Isaiah 42:6–7:**
>
> [6] "I am the Lord; I have called you[a] in righteousness;
>   I will take you by the hand and keep you;
> I will give you as a covenant for the people,
>   a light for the nations,
> [7] to open the eyes that are blind,
> to bring out the prisoners from the dungeon,
>   from the prison those who sit in darkness.

_____
_____
_____
_____
_____

LESSON 5:
RESULTS OF "WALKING IN THE LIGHT" AND OUR CALL TO "GIVE IT AWAY"

As children of the light, what are we called to be? What does that mean, and how do we live this out?

Read Matthew 5:13–16:

Salt and Light

13 "You are the salt of the earth, but if salt has lost its taste, how shall its saltiness be restored? It is no longer good for anything except to be thrown out and trampled under people's feet.

14 "You are the light of the world. A city set on a hill cannot be hidden. 15 Nor do people light a lamp and put it under a basket, but on a stand, and it gives light to all in the house. 16 In the same way, let your light shine before others, so that[a] they may see your good works and give glory to your Father who is in heaven.

_____
_____
_____
_____

Read Matthew 10:26–33:

Have No Fear

26 "So have no fear of them, for nothing is covered that will not be revealed, or hidden that will not be known. 27 What I tell you in the dark, say in the light, and what you hear whispered, proclaim on the housetops. 28 And do not fear those who kill the body but cannot kill the soul. Rather fear him who can destroy both soul and body in hell.[a] 29 Are not two sparrows sold for a penny?[b] And not one of them will fall to the ground apart from your Father. 30 But even the hairs of your head are all numbered. 31 Fear not, therefore; you are of more value than many sparrows. 32 So everyone who acknowledges me before men, I also will acknowledge before my Father who is in heaven, 33 but whoever denies me before men, I also will deny before my Father who is in heaven.

LESSON 5:
RESULTS OF "WALKING IN THE LIGHT" AND OUR CALL TO "GIVE IT AWAY"

What did Jesus say He must be doing? Why? Since Christ is in us and we are now to be the light of the world as His representatives on this Earth, what must we be doing? What does that practically mean for us?

> **Read John 9:1–5:**
>
> Jesus Heals a Man Born Blind
> **9** As he passed by, he saw a man blind from birth. ² And his disciples asked him, "Rabbi, who sinned, this man or his parents, that he was born blind?" ³ Jesus answered, "It was not that this man sinned, or his parents, but that the works of God might be displayed in him. ⁴ We must work the works of him who sent me while it is day; night is coming, when no one can work. ⁵ As long as I am in the world, I am the light of the world."

_____
_____
_____
_____
_____